Don't Give a F**k: Unleash the Power Within You and Become the Best Version of Yourself

The Ultimate Guide on How to Stop Caring About What Other People Think of You

Table of contents

Get your free copy of this eBook:
25 Health Tips to Supercharge Your Life.
Go to *SelfHelpStar.com* to download the book

Introduction

I want to thank you and congratulate you for downloading the book, *"Don't Give a F**k: Unleash the Power Within You and Become the Best Version of Yourself"*.

This book contains proven steps and strategies to help you acquire a new-found sense of confidence, be comfortable in your own skin, and gain a greater degree of self-acceptance as a means of ensuring success and growth in both your personal and professional life.

When you lend an excessive weight to other people's opinion of you, you are in effect limiting the things that you can do. In the process, you reduce your chances for growth because each of your thoughts and actions is preceded by a gnawing fear of being judged.

Your inability to do the things that you should be doing or say the words that you should be saying has a profound effect on your personal happiness and overall sense of well-being. Because you are haunted by your insecurities and doubts, as well as aching for acceptance and validation from others, you actually leave very little room for self-actualization.

The only way you can get out of this is by developing the ability to insulate yourself from the rather unfounded fears of being judged or mocked by others. At their very basic, these fears are nothing more than your own imagined monsters. They prevent you from unleashing your fullest potential, not to mention that they make your life miserable, too.

When you gain a greater appreciation of who and what you are, it becomes easier to put yourself out there and take risks. In the end, it is only by stepping up and being proactive about what you want to achieve that you become the best version of yourself and ultimately be happy.

Thanks again for downloading this book, I hope you enjoy it!

Chapter 1 – Understanding the Human Psyche: Why You Long for Attention and Approval

Humans are inherently social beings. They associate with each other as a means of survival and growth. They live in groups, work in groups, and carry out tasks in groups. The social dynamics of human relations are therefore apparent in almost all aspects of life.

The social nature of being a human manifests itself even in your simplest day to day actions. When you wake up and choose which clothes to wear, for instance, your decision is partly the result of your consideration of how other people are going to look at you in said clothes. Your choice of which dishes to prepare at home is also partly the result of your consideration of the dietary preferences of the members of your household.

Are these considerations wrong? Not necessarily.

If anything, these considerations are deliberately made as a clear display of your appreciation of the necessity of forging healthy ties with the people around you. After all, it is exactly this same sensitivity to the needs and sensibilities of other people that has managed to sustain human relations for a long time.

It is absolutely normal, therefore, to seek approval from others, so long as doing so ensures harmony and peace. The only time this becomes unacceptable is when your need for approval and validation from others begins to get the better of you, resulting in adverse effects to your own quality of life.

The threshold between what is considered acceptable from what is not is difficult to ascertain; it varies from person to person. However, there are a number of common behavioral tendencies that indicate the presence of a problem. You lend an excessive weight to how others think of you when you manifest the following:

1. You find it more convenient and safe to choose the option that the majority takes.

You subscribe to the notion that there is strength in numbers, to the point that you are willing to be left unheard if it means avoiding letting others know that you think differently. You'd rather play it safe and just head where everyone goes instead of going against the flow. You think it's pointless to fight a losing battle. More importantly, you don't want to be seen as a kill-joy and an absolutely humorless weirdo whom everyone hates.

2. In making choices, your primary consideration is what other people are likely going to say and not what you feel you should be doing.

You are always held back from doing or saying things by your nagging fear that you might earn raised eyebrows, or worse, hear rough comments from others. It's almost akin to prior restraint, to use a legal term, where self-expression takes a back seat in light of the possibility of getting prosecuted for it.

3. You'd rather keep quiet than speak up for fear of offending others.

You hate putting others in a compromising or awkward position, in part because of basic courtesy, but mainly because you are not convinced of the validity or legitimacy of your own views. In the greater scheme of things, you think your opinions or actions do not matter as much as the sentiments or feelings of other people.

4. You'd rather suffer in silence than fight for what you believe in because you hate putting yourself in the spotlight.

Nothing makes you uncomfortable more than being required to put yourself out there. You hate to be the subject of comments and criticisms, fair or otherwise. Your greatest fear is to be made fun of, to be the ultimate subject of ridicule, and to lose your face in public. So no matter how unfair you get treated or how bad your end of the bargain is, you'd rather keep mum about it.

5. You take negative criticisms too seriously, to the point of selling out just to avoid getting them whenever possible.

You take criticisms as a form of a personal affront. When someone criticizes you or your work, you regard it as a form of rejection against you and everything you stand for. Your ego and pride get badly bruised each time you hear a negative comment, in part because you have a dismal regard for your own worth, and partly because you think such a criticism could have been easily avoided had you just decided to play safe.

In all these, it is clear that lending an excessive weight to how other people think of you gives rise to a situation where you end up suffering the most. In the process, the biggest casualties are your quality of life, your degree of personal happiness, and your peace of mind.

So how does being a pushover affect your life exactly? This is discussed in greater detail in the next chapter.

Chapter 2 – How Being a Pushover Affects the Way You Live Your Life

You may think that minding other people's opinions about you and adjusting yourself accordingly is no big deal, but you'd be surprised at the degree by which this seemingly benign activity poses an adverse impact on your life.

Experts believe that paying too much attention to what others have to say about you, particularly criticisms that are negative, is a sado masochistic exercise that is ultimately rooted in some unresolved personal issues that you may be harboring. For instance, children who grew up in overprotective homes normally reach adulthood with lesser of the sense of independence and strength of will than their contemporaries who did not grow up in an identical sheltered culture.

Similarly, children who have had to endure repeated verbal abuse from their parents or guardians are believed to grow up with a damaged sense of ego and pride, such that as adults, they are always on the lookout for some semblance of validation or acceptance from other people to compensate for their lonely childhood.

Dismal sense of self-esteem

Regardless, people who can't seem to act or decide on their own without thinking of what others might think of them usually suffer from a dismal sense of self-esteem. These are the sort of people who are willing to bend over and compromise if it meant dodging rejection or criticism from their peers.

Aside from these unresolved personal issues, there are also other reasons that compel people to be overly mindful of what other people might think of them, enough to make them stop on their tracks and think twice before doing anything, if at all.

For instance, there are people who are afraid of taking responsibility for their decisions. They are comfortable taking the safe side, along with the majority, because this set-up prevents them from taking the spotlight should things go awry.

Other people also take the safe side in order to steer clear of confrontations. Even if they think otherwise, they agree anyway to what others decided on, if only to avoid having to take the opposite side and deal with hostile reactions from others.

The tragedy of being a pushover

However, in their avoidance of conflict or disagreements with other people, these individuals end up becoming pushovers. Essentially, pushovers are people who are easy to manipulate or control. They are often taken advantage of for their perceived lack of courage and ability to stand up for themselves. They are the ones frequently picked on because they offer no form of resistance from the abuse they are being subjected to.

In general, unless they can get any form of benefit from them, people do not like to deal with pushovers for a number of reasons. For one, pushovers aren't seen to contribute anything because all they do is agree to everything. Second, pushovers can be annoyingly patronizing, given their propensity to constantly seek for validation and acceptance. And third, pushovers are perennially on their toes, anxious of whether or not each of their actions offends anyone.

Living a life as a pushover can be very stressful, which can ultimately lead to a profound state of unhappiness. When you are unable to live your life on your own terms, you are basically rendering it to a state of uncertainty, improbability, and chance. You take a backseat as you witness your life pass by you without doing anything concrete to turn things around according to your own design. In other words, you let other people dictate how you should live your life.

Chapter 3 – A Life Reinvented: Taking Concrete Steps to Claim Back Your Dignity and Self-Respect

There is nothing dignified about living a life where you are not free to do whatever you want because you are overly concerned about what others might say about you. It's like you always have to censor yourself before doing or saying anything for fear that you might get chastised if you dare.

Now is as good a time as any to change all that.

If you want to reinvent your life and turn things around, a change in mindset should be in order. Altering the way you think and view things is a powerful way to overcome your fears and insecurities, real or imagined.

Begin by considering that in the greater scheme of things, no one really cares about what you do. Even your worst enemy probably has better things to do other than allot much of his or her waking hours devising schemes to humiliate you. As noted author David Foster Wallace once quipped, "You'll worry less about what people think about you when you realize how seldom they do."

In reality, the attention span of people is so short, they'll forget about what you said or did more quickly than you give them credit for. There are a lot of things to do, to see, or to hear for these people to be obsessed with you or any of your imagined shortcomings.

'Much ado about nothing'

In other words, the ultimate lesson to be learned here is that the universe doesn't revolve around you. So when you act like the whole world gives a hoot with every little thing you do or every word you say, you are merely being over-dramatic, for lack of a better term. "Much ado about nothing" is how Shakespeare would have described your regular predicament.

Now that you have disabused yourself from this idea, it is time to focus on the things that you can and should do to ensure that you are not dependent on others for validation. For starters, be firm in what you believe in. There are some things that you should take a stand on, for which you should be able to articulate your position. You cannot simply rely on others to make decisions for you only because you are fearful of making or voicing out your own.

Admittedly, being courageous enough to voice out your opinions, particularly those that run contrary to the majority's, certainly takes a bit of getting used to. As such, regular practice is very important.

Try it with some of your associates when you are discussing things. Instead of simply nodding or saying yes to what others said, feel free to blurt out your thoughts. It may seem awkward and uncomfortable at the beginning, but this can be easily remedied by constant practice. If you do this often, you will realize how speaking up suddenly seems natural and not forced. Apart from developing your ability to muster courage when needed, these little exercises can also help you boost your confidence, improve your conversational skills, and allow you to actively engage in the exchange of ideas rather than merely listen in a corner.

Embracing unpopular ideas

Part of standing up for what you believe in is embracing unpopular ideas. Most times, many people shy away from controversial ideas because they hate to be on the receiving end of a lot of counter-arguments. Fair enough. But what will happen when everyone does the same?

This can be particularly tricky when it comes to dealing with family members. The difficulty arises in the fact that the people you are having disagreements with are not mere strangers, but people whom you are stuck with, for better or for worse, for life. At the same time, the social dynamics in the context of a family are vastly different from ordinary interactions with other people. Emotions, personal histories, and filial connections make it hard to pursue unpopular ideas without the attendant feelings of guilt, remorse, and betrayal.

Of course you don't embrace these unpopular ideas for the sake of being different. You fight for them only when you truly believe in them. Indeed, there can never be enough space for every one's ideas and opinions, no matter how varied they may be, so don't be afraid to speak up.

This applies to other things, too. Apart from opinions on issues, people also have different takes on, say, musical preferences or fashion choices. This is why it's always great to come across people who listen to songs that not many people listen to, or wear clothes that many people wouldn't have the guts of wearing. Their impact is forceful, precisely because of their rarity: not too many people are bold enough to do things their way and not care about what others have to say about them.

Another great thing that you can do to strengthen your free will and practice greater independence is by choosing to travel alone. Traveling is a self-rewarding exercise because by the mere act of traveling, you take yourself out of your comfort zone and instantly subject yourself to challenges of all sorts. With no one to accompany you, you have no one to rely on other than your own instincts, common sense, and rational dictates of your brain. It's a great learning exercise designed to make you realize that you actually have what it takes to get things done.

The next chapter provides a detailed discussion of how you can take full control of your personal and social relations.

Chapter 4 – Taking Full Control of Your Personal and Social Encounters

The moment you choose not to give a f**k about what others think of you, you are in effect giving yourself the opportunity to take full control of your personal and social relations. The freedom to do things on your own, unhampered by baseless fears and self-doubts, fosters an environment conducive for growth and development. By going this route, you are not letting others dictate how you should live your life. The freedom to live your life, as it were, rests solely on your own hands.

Nothing spells freedom more than your capacity to say no. For a long time, you have always been a "yes person" to everything that everyone says. This time, it's going to be different. This time, you will stand by your principles and convictions regardless of how other people are going to take it. This time, you will say what's on your mind because it's the right thing to do. This time, you will choose not to parrot other people's views and instead proudly state your own. This time, you will go against the flow, not just for the sake of going against the tide, but because that's where your heart and mind tell you to do.

Disagreeing without being disagreeable

Also, take an active role in controlling your social environment. If in the past you were made a push-over by the fact that you were constantly around people who thought less of you and felt it proper to boss you around, then it's probably high time to immerse yourself in an altogether new social circle.

Whether you admit it or not, the toxicity of your relationship with your old peers may have aggravated your negative view of yourself. When you are constantly pressured to submission and made the regular subject of derision, you are certainly bound to develop feelings of inferiority.

This time, surround yourself with people with a healthy outlook in life. Be with people to whom you share identical values. Most of all, be in a group that inspires and fosters positivity among its members.

But no matter how well you mix in with other people, there are certainly going to be disagreements at one point or another between yourselves. This is absolutely normal. In such a case, the better frame of mind to adopt is that while you are all entitled to disagree with another, it's an altogether different thing to be disagreeable. How do you do this?

There are two basic social skills you should learn: the first is your ability to deal with awkwardness, and the second is your ability to diffuse tension.

Handling disagreements

As has been discussed in the previous chapters, one of the principal reasons why others lend too much weight on what others might think about them is that they are fearful of enduring awkwardness. Instead of being true to themselves, they choose to adopt the popular opinion because they are scared that to do otherwise would result in a situation where they would have to be on the defensive.

Learning how to deal with awkwardness is therefore something you should be good at. In a nutshell, this involves the capacity to remain calm even in the face of a difficult, potentially explosive, situation.

Related to this is the necessary skill of diffusing tension. When emotions run high and the parties involved are in varying degrees of agitation, a simple disagreement can easily blow up into a major mess. Being diplomatic, refusing to bait or provoke others, or just being sensitive are some of the things that you can subscribe to in this regard.

And finally, a great way of preparing yourself against possible hostile reactions to your words or actions is by conjuring up worst-case scenarios in your head. Suppose you disagree with the idea of, say, a peer at work, what's the worst thing that could happen? You'll probably be asked to substantiate your disagreement and explain why you're taking a different position. In addition, you'll probably be asked to provide your own ideas as to how to address the principal issue at hand. Ask yourself: Can you handle both scenarios? Are you capable of being in the spotlight, open to criticism, as you defend your views? Conjuring up worst case scenarios like these can serve as effective mechanisms for you to prepare yourself.

Chapter 5 – Sustaining Your New-found Sense of Confidence and Positivity Over the Long Term

Choosing not to care about what others might think of you is a lifestyle choice. It is a deliberate and a willful decision made as a means of improving the quality of your life. Such a decision is also geared toward fostering an improved sense of emotional and mental well-being on your part. It is, in other words, a commitment that you have to live by over the long term.

In living up to the demands of this lifestyle choice, it is necessary to sport a certain degree of consistency in your ways. On this end, your ability to shut off negative criticisms and comments should be directed to all aspects of your life. Your ultimate focus should be on the doing, and not on how others perceive such act.

Is this completely attainable? For the most part, it probably is, but certainly not in the absolute sense. You can't live in a protective bubble at all times and guarantee immunity for yourself from any form of negative feedback. So what can you do then?

Taking criticisms with an open mind

Given that you cannot completely do away with criticisms, it's best to take a healthy attitude toward them instead. Take criticisms as a way of identifying aspects about yourself that you can work on and possibly make improvements on. Without such feedback, it would be hard to gauge how you are doing as an individual. As such, it would doubtlessly be more beneficial to take criticisms with an open mind and learn how you can utilize them to your ultimate benefit.

Another thing that you should keep in mind is that dodging responsibility for your actions by always taking the safe side or the stand of the majority isn't going to address the cause of the problem. You cannot play on the safe side at all times without sacrificing your own wants and needs. The aching need to please everyone by packaging yourself as a team player willing to make hard choices at your own expense is not going to fly when it is clear that you are merely being a pushover.

That being said, there is absolutely no way you can please everyone. As such, there is no point in playing the pushover card all the time. The most logical thing to do is to get over your fear of rejection, sport a brave countenance, and embrace the idea that it should be you alone who will be spelling out the terms in your life.

It's alright to be imperfect

And finally, accept your imperfection. When you acknowledge that there are certainly opportunities for improvement in yourself, then it is going to be a lot easier to go about things in your life without unnecessary pressure or burden coming from your end. This is because in most cases, the problem starts when you cannot muster the courage to hear criticisms -- a fault in character that arises from your perception that you can't do no wrong.

Note should be made, though, about the limitations of choosing not to give a f**k to how others think of you. For starters, the sense of freedom that this option affords should not entitle you to be callous, discourteous, or indifferent to other people's thoughts and feelings. While on certain occasions hurting others can't be helped, the need to exercise prudence in your words and actions still remains.

After all, one of the principal reasons why you decided to sport a shift in perspective regarding this aspect of your life is because you wanted to end being treated like a dirt-bag. Instead, you wanted to be treated with respect and dignity. It would therefore be a supreme irony if you yourself were to become the instigator of abuse to other people.

Most importantly, love yourself. It is only by wholeheartedly accepting who and what you are that you can be perfectly capable of standing up for what you believe in. Because in the end, the ultimate measure of your worth as a person is not on the amount of praises or validation your get from other people, but on the respect and love you hold for yourself.

Made in the USA
San Bernardino, CA
16 July 2018